The Top
10
Distinctions Between
Winners
and Whiners

The Top
10
Distinctions Between
Winners
and Whiners

KEITH CAMERON SMITH

WKU Publishing

Published in the United States by WKU Publishing
www.keithcameronsmith.com

ISBN 978-0-9755070-3-2

First Edition

Book design by Mary Jo Zazueta

CONTENTS

The Top
10
Distinctions Between Winners and Whiners

DISTINCTION TEN

Winners take responsibility.

Whiners play the victim.

Let's face it: life doesn't always go according to plan. In fact, it's been said that life is what happens while you're making *other* plans.

To become a winner in the face of this unpredictability requires that you balance two seemingly contradictory ideas. The first is best expressed by the expression *"If it's going to be, it's up to me."* The second is nearly the opposite: *"What will be, will be."*

These two statements sound fine by themselves—but when you put them side-by-side they contradict each other. And yet, taking either of these statements to the extreme produces negative results.

For example, let's look at the first statement: *If it's going to be, it's up to me.* Taking that philosophy to the extreme leads to arrogance and the perception that you don't need anyone. And the second statement? Taken to its extreme, the idea that *What will be, will be* leads to the role of victim, aimlessly drifting with no sense of control.

The truth lies somewhere in the middle. Winners seek to find a balance in life, and the balance point for these two statements is *responsibility*. Responsibility means to do your best and trust that good will happen.

Responsibility means to do your best and trust that good will happen.

You can't always live in a state of *what will be will be*, or you'll never take positive action. You can't always live in a state of *if it's going to be, it's up to me*, or you will think more highly of yourself than you should and become arrogant and judgmental.

These extremes—a lack of perceived control and a state of arrogance—start whiners down a dangerous path that leads to only one place: fear. That sense of fear manifests itself in people as *worry*, and worry is the enemy of winning.

Winners don't worry, whiners do.

Conversely, while fear is faith in the worst that can happen, winners have faith in positive outcomes, and that faith manifests in the form of *trust*—a belief in the good in people and situations.

> Winners don't worry, whiners do.

While there may be people who do not have good intentions towards you, most probably do. Winners look for those who do—and don't worry about the rest.

Winners trust the intentions of others. Whiners play the victim because they allow their fears to grow into worry, their worry to grow into suspicion, and their suspicion to grow into division.

You can't be a winner without others. Life is a team sport. Whining leads to separation, but winning comes only through unity.

You can't be a winner without others. Life is a team sport.

The decision to live by faith or fear is just that: a decision. It is a personal choice and it is one you must make every day.

Your choices are your responsibility. A whiner thinks his choices depend on his circumstances and that those circumstances are someone else's fault.

Fear is rooted in a belief that you have no choice. In reality, your circumstances exist *because* of your choices and those choices are made in the context of either faith or fear. Accept the responsibility to make choices based in faith and you become a winner. Make choices based in fear and you will be a whiner.

Winners know we always have choices, and take responsibility for them. Whiners, however, believe that their choices are controlled by someone else. And while you *can* let someone else control your choices, isn't that a choice in itself? Becoming a winner is impossible until you assume the responsibility of choice. Winners understand that power, and use it wisely.

Whiners play the victim by blaming others for their circumstances. Whiners say, "If only they had done this, or if only they hadn't done that, my life would be perfect." Blaming and complaining go hand-in-hand, and victims do a lot of both.

Remember: *Choices determine my circumstances; circumstances do not determine choices.* As long as you whine about your circumstances you cannot become a winner.

Is there something in your life that you've been blaming others for that has been holding you back? As long as you are blaming and complaining, you are remaining the same. Taking responsibility for your circumstances is the first step to growth.

There have been many situations in my life that I blamed others for. I have learned that

> Taking responsibility for your circumstances is the first step to growth.

as long as I play the victim by blaming and complaining, I battle with feelings of disappointment and discouragement. Once, when I related a disappointment to my friend Nido Qubein, he told me, "Keith, it's okay to be disappointed. It's not okay to be discouraged."

The truth is that we all face disappointment. When we become disappointed, though, we must learn to encourage ourselves before we become discouraged, for beneath discouragement is *depression*.

Whiners battle with depression. Winners deal with their disappointments, encourage themselves, and move on. A winner says, "My thoughts, feelings, and actions are my responsibility."

Winning starts with your thoughts, and taking responsibility for them means choosing positive ones.

> Winning starts with your thoughts, and taking responsibility for them means choosing positive ones.

Whining is the fruit of negative thinking. Don't let others fill your mind with negative thoughts. Make conscious choices on what you hold in your mind, for what you allow to stay there makes you either a winner or a whiner.

Winners choose to be winners. Winners take responsibility for the thoughts, feelings, and actions that produce their circumstances. Whiners let others control their thoughts, and then blame them for the results.

Winners take responsibility.

Whiners play the victim.

DISTINCTION NINE

Winners can have what they want.

Whiners want what they cannot have.

What do you want? Are you willing to pay the price to get it? Everything has a price, and while whiners want something for nothing, winners work hard in pursuit of their passions.

Sometimes hard work is part of the price we pay to get what we want. At other times, things come to us easily and without much effort, and the price we pay is humility, which is to "let go and let God."

There have been times in my life when I have taken my hands off the metaphorical wheel and said, "This is beyond me right now. I don't know how to make this happen yet." Lo and behold, it seems to happen automatically.

Winners know when to press on and when to let go. Whiners press on—until the first obstacle—but instead of trusting that the right outcome will happen, they let go.

Winners let go and trust. Whiners let go and fear.

Whiners believe that other people should provide for them. They feel that because others have more, they are entitled to some of it.

This entitlement-mentality is extremely destructive and leads whiners to a state of self-pity, where they live in a constant quest for sympathy and focus all their energy on how hard life is and why they can't do this or that.

Winners, on the other hand, look at people who have more than them and believe, "If others can do it, so can I." Then, they learn what they need to do to get it.

Most wealthy people weren't handed their wealth—they earned it. Winners understand that they can learn to acquire what they desire.

> Winners . . . look at people who have more than them and believe, "If others can do it, so can I."

You can learn to earn whatever amount of money you desire. You can learn how to be healthy. You can learn how to have deep and meaningful relationships. You can learn to acquire whatever it is you desire.

Part of the price is knowledge. Do you invest in expanding your mind? Are you learning new things? Limitations are simply due to a lack of knowledge.

If you see someone winning in an area where you're losing, it's simply because they know something that you don't know and they are choosing to apply it. You can learn whatever it is you need to know to get *whatever it is that you want*.

> You can learn whatever it is you need to know to get *whatever it is that you want*.

Another price that winners pay to get what they want is criticism. It's windy at the top of the ladder, and criticism can be the price of success. Ironically, whiners are the critics. Because they believe the lie that they can't have something, they criticize those who do have it—whether "it" is wealth, rich relationships, health, or joy.

Whiners are critical because they aren't willing to pay the price of success themselves. Winners pay the price, even when that price is high, and accept that criticism is a part of life. Winners don't care what others think of them. They care what they think of themselves.

How do you feel about yourself? Do you nourish your self-respect? Do you like . . . you? Winners have high self-esteem. But, while they think well of themselves, they are not conceited or arrogant, they simply believe in their abilities. Whiners think poorly of themselves, and criticize others because they have a habit of criticizing themselves.

Winners don't listen to the critics, they listen to their hearts. They are not consumed by what others think about them.

A powerful insight to remember is the 20-40-60 Principle:

> "When you're twenty years old, you care what everyone thinks about you. When you're forty years old, you don't care what anyone thinks about you. When you're sixty years old, you finally realize that nobody was thinking about you at all."

People are consumed by their own lives—they aren't thinking about you all the time. Even when someone criticizes you, he isn't thinking about you five minutes later. If you've been worrying about what others think, I have three words for you: *get over it*.

Whiners live in a constant state of negative energy, critical of almost everything, and consumed with their own egos and the opinions of others. Winners know that it's not all about them, and they willingly pay another winner's price—*service*.

> Winners know that it's not all about them, and they willingly pay another winner's price—*service*.

Zig Ziglar once said, "If you help enough other people get what they want, you can have anything you want." Winners have an innate grasp of service and understand that when they serve others from the heart, it's a sign that they are doing things for the right reasons.

Serving people from the head just so you can get what you want may work to a certain degree, but it removes the joy of service—and the joy that comes from serving from the heart is worth more than anything you could possibly desire. Service that flows from the heart is a price that's a joy and a privilege to pay.

Whiners can't have what they want because of ignorance, low self-esteem, and lack of service. Increase your knowledge about what you do want, ignore criticism, and serve people from your heart—and you can have what you want.

Winners can have what they want.

Whiners want what they cannot have.

DISTINCTION EIGHT

Winners find a way.

Whiners find an excuse.

I once received an e-mail that posed this question: *Which is more important, the power of belief or the power of persistence?*

My immediate response was that belief was more important than persistence. In fact, it is belief that *creates* persistence. It can be challenging to persevere, especially when we're faced with failure, rejection, or loss; but belief gives us the confidence we need to persist in the face of those unexpected barriers.

Henry Ford once said, "If you think you can or you think you can't, you're right." It's a deeper truth than most people realize.

Whiners continue to find excuses for two reasons. First, because things get tough; and second, because they don't believe they can prevail.

It takes a winner to "keep on keeping on" when something goes wrong. A winner sees a setback as a message to learn something new. He resolves to find a way because he believes there *is* a way. Whiners find an excuse because they don't believe they can succeed.

Consider a fly trapped in a room. The fly desperately bangs against the window trying to get free. His struggle is vigorous but futile, and he eventually dies. Why? It seems that the fly has only one strategy: *try harder*. Had the fly simply looked around, he would have noticed that just across the room was an open door— within a few seconds of flying, he could have been free.

Many whiners behave like the fly. They try harder and harder with the wrong strategy. They find either an excuse to keep doing what they're doing or they find an excuse to quit; and in both cases, their behavior is a reflection of their limiting beliefs.

Whiners look at what they are doing and develop beliefs about whether their actions are right or wrong.

Winners look at their results and, if their results are not what they want, they find different ways of being and doing, until they get the results they *do* want. Winners don't judge their actions as right or wrong. They focus on the results and keep adjusting their actions until they create what they want. Whiners either stay on an unsuccessful course or set a new course each time a small challenge arises.

> Winners don't judge their actions as right or wrong. They focus on the results and keep adjusting their actions until they create what they want.

You can find a way to get whatever it is you want, but I challenge you to first discover the kind of *person* you want to be. Focusing on *who* you want to be first, empowers you to find a way to create *what* you want to do and have.

I wanted to be a best-selling author and empower people with simple truths that transform their lives. Although I wrote a book, I went through several years of struggle and some disappointments. But, because I had decided *who* I wanted to be first, I found a way. I persevered, believed I could, and I did.

So, who do you want to be? Winners answer that question before they decide what they want to do or have.

Winners focus on being powerful and peaceful. They feed their faith and starve their fears. They understand that what they do and have is a reflection of who they are. Whiners find an excuse because they don't have a vision for who they want to be. Your vision for yourself and your life must be something you can believe in with all your heart—a vision that fills you with passion and keeps you on course.

Because whiners lack that vision, most of what they do is short-term and devoid of power and commitment. Vision empowers you to find a way, no matter what. A lack of vision helps you only to find an excuse.

Whiners find an excuse because more often than not they are fulfilling someone else's vision and the dreams of others can only inspire for a limited time. It's not wrong or bad to help someone else with their vision; but in order to have long-term passion and inspiration you must personalize it and make it your vision, too.

You *can* make someone else's vision yours and become a winner, and in my experience, a time will come when you do get your own vision. And, just as you have served someone else's vision for a time, you will find people to help serve your vision when it is time to pursue it. Winners help other winners.

Winners can't help whiners who are unwilling to help themselves. Whiners must first help themselves by deciding "I am going to be a winner." After making a decision with your head and a commitment with your heart to become a winner, you will find a way.

Winners find a way.

Whiners find an excuse.

DISTINCTION SEVEN

Winners brighten a room by entering.

Whiners brighten a room by leaving.

Winners energize people. The excitement about who they are becoming and what they are doing in life makes their enthusiasm a tangible force—it feels good just to be in their presence. Whiners, on the other hand, can be emotional vampires, draining the energy from everyone around them.

Have you ever noticed that winners attract other winners, while whiners cluster with whiners?

Birds of a feather do, indeed, flock together.

If you've made the decision to change from whiner to winner, it's essential to surround yourself with winners as much as possible. A warning though: winners will not spend much time with those who continue to complain. To find and keep the company of winners, you will need to eliminate whining from your life.

If God had made eleven commandments,

the eleventh might have been *Thou shalt not whine*. I have a plaque in my home bearing that inscription, and it acts as a constant reminder that although we are all human and we live in a world that can be more pessimistic than opti-

> If God had made eleven commandments, the eleventh might have been *Thou shalt not whine*.

mistic, we must be vigilant in choosing the words we speak.

Whiners brighten a room by leaving because they take their complaining with them. Have you noticed that whiners will actually get into a competition to see whose life is worse? No wonder winners refuse to spend time with whiners.

It's my opinion that the overwhelming majority of people fit the description of a whiner. Even my ninety-six-year-old great-grandmother thinks so. While at my parents' house, dropping off a copy of the Random House version of my book *The Top Ten Distinctions between Millionaires and the Middle Class*, my great-grandmother walked by the table and picked up the book.

She read the title aloud and then asked me, "Does this tell you how to be a millionaire? How do you do it?"

> Most people are addicted to whining, and it takes conscious effort and daily discipline to stop complaining and to become a winner.

I rattled off a few simple things, like having faith, taking risks, and refusing to complain.

She paused and then said, "Well, there ain't gonna be many people getting there."

My grandmother is right. Most people are addicted to whining, and it takes conscious effort and daily discipline to stop complaining and to become a winner.

Like becoming a millionaire, becoming a winner is a choice. Part of that choice is to stop complaining and start appreciating. Winners brighten a room by showing appreciation for life. They talk about the good things that have happened, are happening, and will happen.

In my Wisdom Creates Freedom workshop I give everyone a life-changing challenge—if you're willing to receive it, I'd like to offer it to you. The challenge is this: for seven days, do not complain. If you go one day and then complain on the second day, you must start over at day one. If you go three days without complaining, and complain on the fourth, you must again

> Most people are addicted to whining, and it takes conscious effort and daily discipline to stop complaining and to become a winner.

go back to day one and start over. When you can go seven days without complaining, you will have become very aware of the power of your words. You will also start to notice the winners and whiners in your life on a deeper level.

Whiners are unconscious of how much they whine. Winners are aware of the power of their words, and through those words they brighten a room.

Winners are aware of the power of their words . . .

In addition to complaining, whiners are also masters of self-pity. Winners do not attend pity parties. They don't throw them for themselves and they don't respond to an invitation to attend someone else's.

Self-pity is part of the darkness that leaves a room when a whiner walks out.

It's impossible to become a winner and wallow in self-pity. Wallowing in self-pity is like a dog eating its own vomit or a pig rolling around in its own waste. It's no wonder winners don't spend much time with whiners. Would you want to spend a lot of time with someone who smells like vomit or crap? The reason that whiners can hang out with whiners is because they all smell the same and they are used to the stench.

Winners do, however, spend some time with whiners trying to help them clean themselves off. I love the fact that Jesus took time to be with whiners and influence them for the good. Winners work with whiners until they can tell that the whiner is not willing to grow. If a whiner is committed to staying the same—well, let's just say that there is only so much of the smell that a winner can take.

You might say that winners make a room smell better by entering and whiners make a room smell better by leaving. How do you smell? What do winners pick up on when they are around you? Are you aware of your light and your darkness?

We all have the potential to brighten a room or darken it. Winners focus on walking in light. They are appreciative and focus more on the good in this world than the bad. They brighten a room by encouraging others, congratulating others, and refusing to speak poorly of others. Whiners discourage others, compete with each other on how bad their lives are, and gossip.

> [Winners] are appreciative and focus more on the good in this world than the bad. They brighten a room by encouraging others, congratulating others, and refusing to speak poorly of others.

Becoming a winner demands that you focus on the positive. Winning is a choice. Choose to appreciate, encourage, and find the good in yourself and others. Choose to be a winner and help light the way for those that follow.

Winners brighten a room by entering.

Whiners brighten a room by leaving.

DISTINCTION SIX

Winners listen twice as much
as they talk.

Whiners talk twice as much
as they listen.

You may be surprised to discover that the greatest communication skill you can master has nothing to do with talking. The greatest communication skill you can master is to *listen*.

By learning to be a committed listener you can develop deeper and more meaningful relationships. When you focus your attention on listening to *understand* rather than listening to respond, you learn more, connect better, and the conversation reaches a deeper level.

> By learning to be a committed listener you can develop deeper and more meaningful relationships.

The tendency in our society is to interrupt people while they are talking. Someone says something that triggers a thought in our minds, and we feel a need to blurt that thought out. As soon as we *think* we know what they are saying, we interrupt to share our opinions or beliefs about the topic. Sadly, though, when we interrupt people like this, we usually miss what they are really trying to say.

Winners learn to listen and they continually work to master the skill. Whiners can't keep their mouths shut. They ramble on and on, oblivious to how many times they interrupt others. Pay attention during your next conversation. How often do you feel a need to cut short the speech of others? Do you interrupt people more than you sincerely listen to them?

If you reflect for a moment, you will find that when you speak with someone that you really admire—someone you truly respect—you tend to listen more than you talk. The lesson here is not that you shouldn't interrupt people you respect—after all, winners respect all people equally—but that when you interrupt, *you com-*

municate a lack of respect to the person you are speaking to.

Another critical distinction is that winners listen with their hearts, while whiners listen only with their *heads*. Our cognitive processes—our "heads"—are reactive and dominated by our ego. That ego is proud of what we think we know, and wants to prove it. When we use our emotional intelligence—our "hearts"—to listen, we connect with others on a more profound level. We try to truly understand what they are feeling and saying, not what we *think* they are saying. Winning relationships are formed by those who practice listening with their hearts; the inability to grasp this distinction is at the root of countless failed marriages and business partnerships.

When you become a committed listener, you are becoming a winner. Here's another challenge for you. For the next seven days, commit to being a *listener* in every conversation you have. Resist the urge to interrupt, or even speak. Just listen with your heart. You'll find that this challenge will also help with the challenge of not complaining—after all, if you're talking less you'll probably be complaining less. So, for seven days, don't complain and practice being a committed listener. These two simple challenges will put you on the path of a winner.

Have you ever wondered why God gave us two ears and one mouth? I think that it's a clear message that we should listen twice as much as we talk. Most people are addicted to talking and do quite the opposite—they talk at least twice as much as they listen. What causes this imbalance?

Once again, we find ego at the root of the problem. Many people try desperately to prove their points at any cost, and persuade others to see their opinions as right. Some people can't stand it when others disagree with them. And, although it is nice when people agree with us, winners understand that people have their own opinions and trying to talk someone into a new point of view isn't the wisest use of time.

It's funny to me that if you let a whiner talk and talk and talk, you can watch them confuse themselves and then try to make sense out of what they just said.

Whiners are good at justifying their beliefs and finding reasons why they are right and we are wrong. Whiners don't have deep relationships because their communication is so shallow. Even in conversation with others, whiners are usually having a monologue not a dialogue. Whiners are so stuck in their own perceptions that it's extremely difficult for them to consider what someone else is saying, especially if it differs from their opinions.

This distinction reveals a simple, yet very profound, secret to success: *talk less and listen more*. If you do this, then you will start learning more and seeing the world differently, which leads to new experiences and ideas.

Talking less and listening more is a great way to increase your inner peace. Peace is a powerful state, one that leads to prosperity. If you want to increase your peace and decrease your stress, talk less.

> If you want to increase your peace and decrease your stress, talk less.

Listening more attentively to others will also empower you to listen more to your own heart. That small still voice that we call "gut feeling" or "intuition" becomes clearer and easier to hear when you are quiet. Talk less and listen more—

you may even be surprised to hear your heavenly Father communicate with you. When you are in a conversation, say only what you really need to say and then simply listen.

Winners listen twice as much
as they talk.

Whiners talk twice as much
as they listen.

DISTINCTION FIVE

Winners enjoy life's journeys.

**Whiners put their joy in
the destinations.**

Life is a series of journeys and destinations. Winners enjoy them both, but if you learn to find joy in the journey, you will experience a lot more of it. The joy of reaching a destination lasts only for a brief moment.

People tend to focus on where they're going. When they get there, though, they feel good for about a minute and then start looking for another destination. Learn to enjoy where you are. Yes, keep climbing, but don't make all of your joy dependent on achievement—make a decision to be happy here and now. Don't put your happiness off until a point in the future, for that is a great deception. If you think you will be happy tomorrow, remember that tomorrow never arrives.

> Don't put your happiness off until a point in the future, for that is a great deception. If you think you will be happy tomorrow, remember that tomorrow never arrives.

Winners live in the present. They have goals and plans for the future; but they have learned to take action now with joy. Joy is strength for the journey. It empowers us to keep going, even when we are tempted to quit. Whiners quit easily because they don't allow the power of joy to flow until they achieve or arrive.

Since whiners put their joy off until they achieve something or arrive somewhere, they walk through life in a weakened condition. The weakness causes a lack of perseverance. Whiners tire and give up because they just don't have the energy. Joy is energy to finish the journeys of life, and joy is a choice.

> Joy is energy to finish the journeys of life, and joy is a choice.

There are a many journeys in life and we often find ourselves on more than one at the same time. School is a journey. Marriage is a journey. Parenting is a journey. Your career is a journey. Going on vacation can be a journey. Losing a loved one is a journey. Financial freedom is a journey. There are hundreds of journeys we can take in our lifetime. The key to finishing them is to make each journey with joy.

Fortunately, enjoying the journeys as well as the fleeting moments of the destinations is something we can all choose to learn. Here are three keys to help you experience the joy of the journey: *growing*, *gratitude*, and *focus*.

> . . . three keys to help you experience the joy of the journey: *growing, gratitude,* and *focus.*

Growing

I believe growing is one of the main purposes of life. We are not happy if we are not becoming the best we can be. If you're in school, for example, then you should be growing in specialized knowledge. If you're in a marriage, then you should be growing in love and understanding. We grow in different areas at different times in our lives.

Life demands growth; and each time we try to stay the same, we experience pain, not joy. If you are on a parenting journey, then you should

> . . . growing is one of the main purposes of life.

be growing as an example of wisdom, and becoming aware that your attitude and actions are affecting the journeys of your children.

In truth, our attitude and actions probably affect more people's journeys than we realize. If you are taking a short journey called a vacation, you can be learning how quick life goes and how quick the joys of destinations are gone.

If you are taking the journey called losing a

loved one, you can grow in understanding how precious life is and learn to build deeper relationships with those who are still with you.

Winners grow and experience joy. Whiners try to stay the same and experience pain.

Gratitude

Think of something or someone that you are thankful for right now. Seriously, do it right now—and then notice how you feel. Gratitude affects our mood. Gratitude generates joy. If you want to increase your joy for the journeys of your life, then increase your gratitude. Winners cultivate gratitude in their lives as one of the fastest and greatest ways to experience joy.

Focus

What you focus on is what you feel. Focus on the good in your journey and you'll feel good. Focus on the bad and you'll feel bad. This power of focus is the power to control your feelings.

Your mind can only hold one thought at a time, so make it a good one. Every journey contains some good you can focus on. Even during the loss of a loved, we can focus on appreciating our family and friends. We can focus on the good memories we have. We always have a choice of where we direct our focus. And where we direct it determines whether we experience joy or pain.

> Every journey contains some good you can focus on.

So, as you experience your journey, keep growing, cultivating gratitude, and focusing on the good. Make joy your responsibility; do not be dependent on other people or destinations. Winners create joy right where they are. The present moment is all that exists—learn to live in it. Focusing too much on the past or future steals your joy. Whiners live their lives regretting the past and fearing the future more than they live in the present.

Winners create joy right where they are.

The rare moments of joy that whiners experience occur because they briefly become aware of the present moment. Winners continually practice being present because they know that is where their strength and joy flow from.

Being present allows you to enjoy the journeys and the destinations of life. Being absent creates suffering and pain. When you focus too much on the destination, you miss the beautiful moments of your life. Learn to enjoy the journey. Grow, be thankful, and focus on the good.

Winners enjoy life's journeys.

Whiners put their joy in the destinations.

DISTINCTION FOUR

Winners build friendships.

Whiners destroy friendships.

Friendships are one of the most valuable and precious things that we can possess in this life. What does it mean to be a friend? It means to look out for the best interests of another human being. Of course, problems in friendships occur when friends have different opinions of what those best interests are.

True friends will do whatever they can to work through their differences. Have you ever had a friend become angry with you because you didn't agree with him? Have you ever gotten angry at a friend because of a misunderstanding? People have different perceptions and opinions and, as a result, we have misunderstandings.

Winners understand this and choose to work through their differences instead of becoming angry about them. A classic example is when a husband and wife are talking and the husband is not hearing what his wife is really saying, or vice-versa. Later, one will say to the other, "I asked you to do this," and the other will say, "No, you didn't." Within moments, the situation deteriorates into anger.

We do not always hear what other people are trying to communicate to us. True friends respect each other and listen with their hearts.

Winners are able to build deep and meaningful friendships because they acknowledge that their friends have *perceptions* and *opinions*.

A perception is the way you see or understand something. An opinion is a belief you have, based on your past results. If you want to build more friendships, then acknowledge that perceptions and opinions are not absolute truths. Just because we see things differently doesn't mean that we are right, even if our ego demands it.

Winners don't immediately assume they are right. Winners practice looking at situations from different perspectives. Whiners, on the other hand, almost always assume that their way is the only way.

Ego has destroyed millions of friendships. It is impossible to build long-lasting friendships without humility. Humility is the ability to learn and grow. Humility is the willingness to let someone be as they are and accept them that way. It is the power to love people unconditionally. Humility is a willingness to forgive. All long-lasting friendships are built on humility and forgiveness. And, while we will always have misunderstandings in our friendships, win-

> All long-lasting friendships are built on humility and forgiveness.

ners know this and choose to build stronger friendships when they occur. Humility is the secret to friendships, and it is the key to becoming a winner.

We've all had moments when we thought we were right, but later, upon reflection or more information, we acknowledged we were wrong. Our perceptions and opinions are limited. The more you hold onto your way of seeing and believing, the more difficult it will be to build friendships.

> The more you hold onto your way of seeing and believing, the more difficult it will be to build friendships.

When we try to demand that someone else change his perception and see things as we do, we have stopped being a friend and started to become arrogant.

Arrogance is an unwillingness to even consider another perspective, and whiners destroy friendships because of it. Ego is rooted in arrogance, and when whiners allow their egos to run their lives, it ruins their lives, too.

Winners know when to be dependent, independent, and interdependent. There are times when things are beyond our control and we must depend on others; and there are times when our friends need to lean on us. Then, there are times when we need to stand on our own two feet. Wisdom is knowing exactly *when* to be dependent, independent, and interdependent.

> Winners know when to be dependent, independent, and interdependent.

There are also times when we need others and they need us. Learning when to be interdependent is a key to being a winner. Interdependency is what friendship is all about.

It is where miracles can occur. Being interdependent allows the wisdom and knowledge of both people to flow freely, allowing great things to happen.

Whiners don't know much about being interdependent. They are usually dependent victims or independently arrogant. Being interdependent is where love, humility, and forgiveness flow. It is an understanding that I have something to contribute and so do you. It is balance between needing each other and wanting each other. Interdependence focuses on what is best for everyone. Whiners want things on their terms. Winners want what is best for all. Winners are other-people minded and inclusive. Whiners are selfish and exclusive.

Look closer at the word *friendship*. It is made of two words, friend and ship. When two or more people get in a ship going in the same direction, their path is one of unity and peace. When two or more people want to go in different directions, there is only division and stress.

A key to building friendships is to find the things you agree on. Accept the fact that there are things that you are not going to agree on, but focus on what you do agree on. That focus leads to smooth sailing away from the storms of disagreement that destroy friendships.

Winners build friendships.

Whiners destroy them.

DISTINCTION THREE

Winners think big.

Whiners think small.

Most of us have been trained from the time we were very young to think small—we've been taught only to survive, and survival thinking is narrow in its focus. When you shift your focus beyond survival, to the larger goal of *freedom*, you will find your thinking will expand, too.

Thinking big requires a conscious choice, and once we begin to make this choice on a consistent basis, we begin to understand how limiting our perceptions have been. When we choose to think bigger, we start to see possibilities, and our perceptions and opinions begin to transform.

Faith is the belief in good things happening, and thinking big is the fruit of that faith. By exercising your faith, you experience positive feelings and emotions. Thinking big produces excitement and joy. Thinking small produces fear and anxiety. Fear is to believe that bad things are going to happen. Small thinking is the

Faith is the belief in good things happening, and thinking big is the fruit of that faith.

fruit of fear. Winners exercise their faith by taking action towards their deep desires. Whiners live in fear and ignore their dreams and goals.

I believe everyone has a big dream. Winners pursue theirs with belief that it can be achieved. Since whiners think small, they doubt that their big dream is possible. Their lack of faith can be seen in the difference between the questions that winners and whiners ask themselves. For example, winners ask, "How can I?" while whiners ask, "Can I?"

Winners assume they can, they just need to learn *how*. Whiners want to believe they can, but their small thinking and doubts prevent it. They ask, "Can I?" because there is an underlying fear that they *can't*. It's always a mistake to assume the negative—if you're going to make assumptions, make them positive ones. Ask yourself, "How can I achieve my big dream?"

Believe that your big dream is possible. Have faith in it. By focusing on your big dream with faith, you will start thinking bigger.

Faith, like fear, is a choice; and we learn to choose fear at a very young age. Winners have a time in their lives when they are confronted with their fears and they choose to have faith and pursue their purposes with passion. Whiners meet their fears and retreat back to a life of small living.

If you struggle with fear, doubts, and small thinking, understand that these are only perceptions, and that perceptions can be changed. Just because you hold a belief now, doesn't mean you have to hold that belief forever. We can change our beliefs. We can alter our opinions. Winners are not afraid to question what they believe and see if their belief is limiting them. Winners understand that beliefs influence our behaviors and our behaviors influence our results. They look at their results and if they are not what they want, they go to work on their beliefs.

Whiners assume their beliefs are right and blame their results on someone or something else. Remember, *your results are your responsibility*. If they are not what you want, then work on expanding your beliefs. Think bigger. Expand your perception of what is possible. The reason that whiners continue to think small is because they keep the same beliefs.

Thinking big will require you to change your beliefs. Winners work on their thoughts. Thinking is the process of asking yourself questions. Winners learn to ask themselves bigger questions which, of course, delivers bigger answers. By asking new and bigger questions, we come up with new ideas of what is possible. Big questions expand our minds to the point that we find things we used to think were impossible are now within our grasp. (I have written in detail about this concept in *The Top Ten Distinctions between Millionaires and the Middle Class*.) Whiners are rigid in their beliefs. They refuse to consider things that are different from what they already believe, and so they remain whiners. The only way for a whiner to become a winner is to think bigger.

Thinking bigger requires new beliefs of what is possible. Thinking big requires faith, bigger questions, and new beliefs. Choose

> Thinking big requires faith, bigger questions, and new beliefs.

to have that faith, to ask yourself those bigger questions, and to work on expanding your beliefs.

Winners think big.

Whiners think small.

DISTINCTION TWO

Winners are focus-minded.

Whiners are scatterbrained.

Have you ever felt overwhelmed, or experienced the anxiety of having too much coming at you at once? We all have, at one time or another, and during those moments the stress of being overwhelmed reduces our ability to think, create, and make decisions.

There are two significant causes for feeling overwhelmed. The first is *complaining*. When you complain, you play the victim, talk excessively, destroy friendships, and think small. Whining overwhelms people and destroys peace of mind.

Remember that winners don't whine and whiners don't win. Winners live with peace of mind. Whiners live in a near-constant state of feeling overwhelmed.

The second source for feeling overwhelmed is being *scatterbrained*. As long as you are scatterbrained you will be stressed. When you learn to focus on your top priorities, your mind becomes quiet and you find yourself at peace. A focused mind is powerful and can create new ideas to solve problems.

Ideas can flow from a focused mind. A scattered brain is weak and starts to shut down. For a scattered brain, creativity is next to impossible.

Our minds can only handle a limited number of things. While some people may be able to juggle ten or more things at a time, others may only be able to deal with two or three. When we try to focus on more than we are capable of, we feel overwhelmed.

The solution is to simplify your life.

Winners simplify their lives by breaking them down into categories. Whiners complicate their lives by thinking in terms of all and everything. What are your priorities in each area of life? What are your spiritual priorities? What are your emotional priorities? What are your mental priorities? What are your physical priorities? What are your financial priorities?

Start with your responsibilities. What are you responsible for? It is my experience that we often take responsibility for things that we shouldn't and neglect the things we should. Overwhelm is deceptive because it comes even when we are trying to do a lot of good things. We can't do everything. We can't even do everything that we want to do; but we can do everything that we need to do. We get so scatter-brained by trying to do too much. Sometimes our desires create enormous amounts of stress for us because we think we have to fulfill them. We don't.

Sometimes you bounce your focus around from things that you regret in the past, to fears you have about the future, to the things demanding your attention right now. When you are overwhelmed, you are living in reaction. To become a winner, you need to move from reaction to *creation*.

> To become a winner, you need to move from reaction to *creation*.

In those moments of feeling overwhelmed, it is critical to reprioritize your life by asking yourself, "What is really important right now?" You have to find out how many things you can juggle and still maintain your peace. After you know that, then focus your mind on the most important things. If you can handle seven things at a time without feeling overwhelmed, then find the top seven things you need to focus on and let go of the rest. Focus on what's most important right now.

You can either use your mind by focusing it—or be used by it by being scatterbrained.

There are some things you think you want,

but once you get them you realize that they weren't what you wanted after all. Desires have the potential to drive people crazy, and it's critical to learn to discern between what you really want and need versus what you think would make you happy.

If you focus your mind on what's really important, you'll find that you can live quite well with less. The push for more and more in our society is destroying millions of lives. Learn to simplify and find the few things that truly bring you peace. Peace is not found in the hurry and worry of our society. It's found by focusing your mind on what is *most* important to you.

Winners are focus-minded.

Whiners are scatterbrained.

DISTINCTION ONE

Winners create positive meanings.

Whiners create negative meanings.

How do you define the seasons, events, and moments of your life? How do you view the circumstances and people around you? Winners have learned to look for and find the good in their lives and the world. Whiners seek—and eventually find—the negative aspects of their lives.

One of the most powerful things you can learn to do is create positive meanings. Even for seemingly negative events, there exists a silver lining. Seek it, and you shall find it. What are you seeking? The good or the bad?

You get what you look for in life. It's worth repeating: *You get what you look for in life.* Most people take the seasons, events, and moments of their lives and define them as negative. Even when life offers them a wonderful opportunity, they miss it. Why? *Because they simply aren't looking for it.*

Winners find the opportunity in every difficulty because they seek

> You get what you look for in life.

it. Whiners find the difficulty in every opportunity because they, too, find what they seek.

What is your initial mental reaction when faced with a difficult experience? Do you look for the good or the bad? Almost every event in our lives can be viewed as negative or positive. Why not choose the empowering path?

Whiners view the world through a negative lens, a damaging perspective that creates needless suffering. And, although suffering can bring its own positive lessons into our lives, whiners experience needless mountains of self-inflicted struggle and pain. The meanings you create in your life determine whether you experience joy or pain. They have the power to get you through the tough times and they also have the power to keep you stuck for a long time. How do you define your experiences?

One of the most destructive things I see whiners do is stack several events of their lives and create negative meanings for each one. Another way to ruin your life is to define entire seasons of your life as negative. Many people do this in business and marriage. They look back on a season, remember a few negative moments, and label the entire season as negative.

Winners remember the good times from their past. They even think back to some of the tough times with gratitude—because they learned so much going through them. Most seasons have both positive and negative experiences in them—choose to remember the positive moments. In your present moments, learn to call them good. If you're going through a tough time right now, is it possible that it contains a hidden blessing? Yes, it's very possible. Strive to create positive meanings in your present circumstances. As you do this more and more, you will think back on these moments with joy and gratitude.

In my book *The Top 10 Distinctions between Millionaires and the Middle Class,* the number one distinction is that millionaires ask themselves empowering questions while the middle class asks themselves disempowering questions. People will remain whiners as long as they ask disempowering questions and create negative meanings. When you learn to ask yourself empowering questions and create positive meanings, then you will become a winner.

> When you learn to ask yourself empowering questions and create positive meanings, then you will become a winner.

There is one specific question that we

always (yes, always) ask ourselves during an experience. The question is: *What does this mean?* Most people are unaware of the questions and answers that are continually going through their minds, but winners are conscious of this inner dialogue. They create empowering questions and positive answers. Learn to duplicate that, and your life will be transformed. You will move from fear to faith, from stress to peace, from darkness to light. Whatever you are going through, find the good.

Winners create positive meanings.

Whiners create negative meanings.

What Now?

Read this book often. I recommend reading it once a month until you feel the ten distinctions have become a part of who you are. Repetition is the primary way we train our minds to think differently. When we think differently, we act differently and achieve different results.

Share copies of this book with the important people in your life so you can discuss the distinctions and learn from one another's experiences and perspectives.

Go to www.keithcameronsmith.com and register for the Wise Distinctions email to receive continued support in developing your mindset for a positive attitude and success.

You can also join me for teleseminars and get information about upcoming Wisdom Creates Freedom workshops.

About the Author

KEITH CAMERON SMITH is an entrepreneur and inspirational speaker who teaches his financial success principles to individuals and companies around the country. The author of The Spiritual Millionaire, The Top 10 Distinctions between Millionaires and the Middle Class, and other books, Smith lives in Ormond Beach, Florida, with his wife and two children.

Visit his website: keithcameronsmith.com

For more information, please visit:

www.keithcameronsmith.com